ICELAND
THROUGH THE AGES

A Concise Guide

By

Martin Miller-Yianni

COPYRIGHT AND ACKNOWLEDGEMENTS

Publisher: Martin Miller-Yianni, Yambol, Bulgaria

First Printing Edition 2024

ISBN 978-619-7742-43-5 (paperback)
ISBN 978-619-7742-44-2 (ePub)

A CIP catalogue record for this book is available from:

The National Register of Published Books in Bulgaria
bulevard 'Vasil Levski' 88,
1504 Sofia,
Bulgaria

Cover Photograph (Kirkjufell, Iceland)
By Zak Boca via Unsplash

Title Page Image by The Author (via Copilot Designer)

"Iceland Through the Ages: A Concise Guide" is a meticulously crafted volume that offers a captivating exploration of Iceland's rich historical background. This book is part of a series of books about the history of various countries. All books in the series are authored in British English, with a keen eye for detail and a commitment to accuracy and stand as a beacon of important historical information while remaining accessible to readers of all backgrounds.

One of the book's notable strengths lies in its ability to provide a comprehensive overview without sacrificing depth. Each chapter delves into the nuances of Iceland's diverse historical foundations, offering readers a clear understanding of the forces that have shaped the nation over the centuries.

A particularly commendable aspect of the book is its approach to handling transitions between historical eras. Recognising the interconnectedness of Iceland's history, the author deftly navigates era shifts by providing recaps and explanations of key events. These recapitulations not only reinforce the continuity of Iceland's historical tale but also serve as valuable aids for readers in grasping the broader historical context.

Whether one seeks to deepen their knowledge of a specific historical period or gain a more general understanding of Iceland's past, the book offers a wealth of reliable information and insightful analysis. From the triumphs and challenges of ancient civilisations to the cultural metamorphoses of more recent times, each chapter immerses readers in the unfolding drama of Iceland's historical evolution and present status quo.

CONTENTS

Chapter 1 - Iceland Before Settlers

Chapter 2 - Settlement Period

Chapter 3 - Commonwealth Era

Chapter 4 - The Icelandic Sagas

Chapter 5 - Union with Norway

Chapter 6 - Reformation and Danish Rule

Chapter 7 - Independence Movement

Chapter 8 - Home Rule

Chapter 9 – The Republic of Iceland

The Icelandic Coat of Arms, known as the "Skjaldarmerkið" or shield, has deep historical and cultural significance for Iceland. Adopted in 1944 when Iceland became a republic, it features a shield with a silver-edged, red cross on a blue background.

The cross's roots trace back to the era of the Vikings, symbolising the Christian faith that has been the country's official religion since the year 1000. Over time, its design evolved, but its essence as a national symbol remained constant.

Today's Icelandic Coat of Arms showcases a bold, vertically oriented cross. Blue represents the sky and the surrounding Atlantic Ocean, while red signifies the volcanic fires the country is known for, and white represents the snow that covers the country in winter.

Despite political changes, the cross endures as a powerful emblem of Iceland's identity, unity, and independence. It proudly adorns official documents, government buildings, and military insignia.

The national flag of Iceland is characterised by its unique and meaningful design. It consists of a blue field with a white-edged red cross that extends to the edges of the flag. The vertical part of the cross is shifted towards the hoist side, following the tradition of Nordic crosses.

This distinctive combination of colours holds deep significance, symbolising the natural elements that have long been integral to Iceland's geographical and cultural identity.

Adopted on June 17, 1944, the flag's inception closely followed Iceland's declaration of independence from Denmark. Beyond its aesthetic appeal, each hue in the flag carries a profound representation of the nation's natural beauty and historical heritage. The blue represents the vast and clear skies as well as the surrounding Atlantic Ocean, the white signifies the snow that covers the country in winter, and the red embodies the volcanic fires the country is known for.

Together, these elements form a powerful emblem of Iceland's identity and aspirations as a sovereign nation.

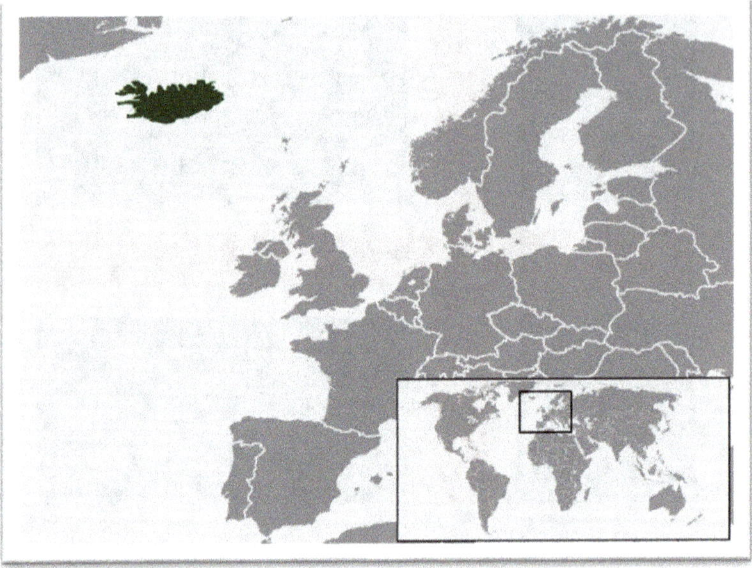

Iceland is located in the North Atlantic Ocean, situated to the northwest of the United Kingdom and to the southeast of Greenland. It is a Nordic Island country that is known for its unique geographical position on the Mid-Atlantic Ridge. The capital and largest city of Iceland is Reykjavik, which is situated in the southwestern part of the country.

The geographical landscape of Iceland is diverse and largely shaped by volcanic activity. It features vast lava fields, geysers, hot springs, and numerous active volcanoes. The country is also known for its large glaciers, with Vatnajökull being the largest in Europe.

The interior mainly consists of a plateau characterised by sand fields, mountains, and glaciers, while many glacial rivers flow to the sea through the lowlands. Iceland's coastline is indented with numerous fjords and inlets, providing a stunning view of the North Atlantic Ocean.

PRE-HISTORY - 9TH CENTURY A.D.

Before the sound of human footsteps trod across its vast landscapes, Iceland was a blank canvas from which nature created its masterpiece. This island, nestled in the North Atlantic Ocean, is a geological marvel, its existence a result of the relentless forces of fire and ice.

VOLCANIC ACTIVITY FORMING ICELAND'S LANDSCAPE

Iceland's birth traces back to the Mid-Atlantic Ridge, a colossal underwater mountain range formed by the divergent boundary of the North American and Eurasian tectonic plates. As these plates drifted apart, magma from the Earth's mantle ascended to the ocean floor, solidifying upon contact with the cold seawater. Over millions of years, repeated volcanic eruptions led to the formation of this land combining the extremes of nature's heat and frozen pastures.

The volcanic activity endowed Iceland with a rugged and desolate beauty. Lava fields, remnants of past eruptions, stretch across vast expanses, their hardened surfaces a testament to the island's fiery origins. Majestic mountains, sculpted by volcanic forces, punctuate the horizon, their peaks often shrouded in mist. The coastline is etched with deep fjords, carved by ancient lava flows meeting the sea.

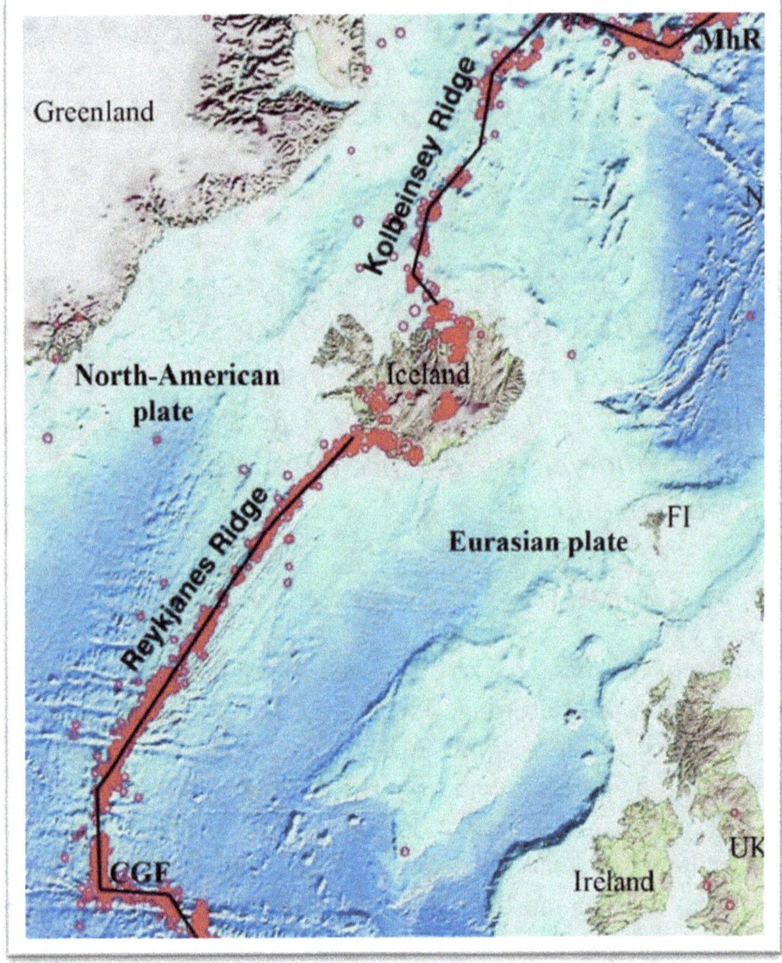

MAP OF THE NORTH AMERICAN AND EURASIAN TECTONIC PLATES

THE ICE AGE SCULPTURING THE LAND

However, Iceland's geological background is not solely a tale of volcanic might. During the ice age, glaciers, the architects of the ice, shaped the land. These colossal ice masses, moving with slow but unstoppable force, carved out valleys and fjords, leaving behind a dramatic landscape when they retreated.

The Highlands, the heart of Iceland, bear the scars of this glacial legacy. This interior wilderness is a realm of black sand deserts and jagged peaks, a stark reminder of the ice ages that once gripped the land.

The interplay of fire and ice has woven a geological wonder across Iceland. Geysers and hot springs, powered by the island's geothermal energy, punctuate the landscape, offering a window into the Earth's fiery heart. Glaciers and ice caps, covering over 10% of the country, stand as frozen sentinels, preserving the legacy of the ice ages.

GEYSERS AND HOT SPRINGS IN SELJALANDSFOSS

The first human chapter in Iceland's history began with the arrival of Norse explorers in the 9th century. Drawn by the promise of new lands, these intrepid seafarers braved the treacherous North Atlantic seas, making Iceland their home and marking the dawn of human civilisation on the island.

Thus, the geological saga of Iceland is a combination of creation and transformation, a story spanning millions of years. It's a tale that continues to unfold, with each passing day adding a new note to the compounds of geological forces that shape this extraordinary island.

SUMMARY:

Iceland, a geological creation in the North Atlantic Ocean, was formed millions of years ago by the divergent boundary of the North American and Eurasian tectonic plates. This led to repeated volcanic eruptions that created a rugged landscape of lava fields, mountains, and fjords. During the ice ages, glaciers further shaped the land, leaving behind a dramatic terrain. The interplay of fire and ice including geysers, hot springs, and glaciers. The first human inhabitants, Norse explorers, arrived in the 9th century. Thus, Iceland's geological saga is a tale of creation and transformation that continues to unfold.

PEOPLE:

Norse Explorers: Overall, a combination of geographical isolation, harsh climate, limited resources, and glacial activity likely contributed to the absence of human habitation on Iceland before the 9th century. It wasn't until Norse explorers braved the treacherous North Atlantic seas and established permanent settlements around 870 A.D. that Iceland's human history began.

PLACES:

Untouched Nature: Before the 9th century, there were no established settlements or significant places of human activity on the island during this time. Instead, Iceland's landscape was shaped by geological forces such as volcanic activity and glacial movements. The natural features of the island, including its rugged terrain, mountains, fjords, and geothermal areas, existed in their pristine state, untouched by human presence.

EVENTS:

Nature's Evolvement: Only nature's events unfolded during this time. Iceland's pristine landscape, shaped by volcanic activity and glacial movements, boasted a dramatic terrain of mountains, fjords, and valleys. Iceland's formation is attributed to the Mid-Atlantic Ridge, where tectonic plates diverged, leading to volcanic eruptions that gradually formed the island's landmass.

9ᵀᴴ – 10ᵀᴴ CENTURIES

The Settlement Period in Iceland, believed to have commenced in the latter half of the 9th century, stands as a pivotal era characterised by the migration of Norse settlers across the North Atlantic.

NORSE SETTLEMENTS

The Norse settlers, primarily originating from Norway, discovered Iceland, a wild and untamed land that was unoccupied and free from the constraints of pre-existing civilisations. This discovery was not a planned expedition, but rather a fortuitous encounter, akin to stumbling upon a hidden treasure.

The motivation behind this mass migration, however, remains a topic of debate and speculation among historians. Some theories suggest that the migration was a result of internal strife within Norway, triggered by the ambitious expansionist policies of the Norwegian monarch, Harald I. Harald's desire to consolidate his rule and establish a unified kingdom is believed to have led to significant unrest and conflict, prompting many to seek new homes elsewhere.

However, contemporary historians often delve deeper, exploring other potential factors that could have contributed to this migratory wave. One such factor is the scarcity of arable land in

Scandinavia. The region's harsh climate and rugged terrain made farming a challenging endeavour, and the growing population would have inevitably led to a strain on resources. This lack of cultivable land could have been a significant push factor, driving the Norse people to venture out in search of new lands to settle and farm.

Moreover, the allure of Iceland, with its vast expanses of untouched wilderness, fertile soils, and abundant resources, would have been a strong pull factor. The prospect of starting anew in a land free from the conflicts and constraints of their homeland would have been an enticing proposition for many Norse settlers.

Thus, the migration to Iceland can be seen as a complex interplay of various push and pull factors, ranging from political unrest and resource scarcity in Norway to the allure of new opportunities and a fresh start in Iceland. This period of migration marked a significant chapter in Norse history, shaping the cultural and demographic landscape of both Norway and Iceland for centuries to come.

PIONEERS OF THE TIME

The trailblazer of this era was undoubtedly Ingólfr Arnarson, who embarked on a journey from Norway to Iceland in the year 874 with the intention of establishing his own settlement. He chose Reykjavík as his place of residence, a decision that would forever mark the city as the first permanent Norse settlement in Iceland.

Ingólfr, along with his wife Hallveig Fróðadóttir, worked tirelessly to cultivate the land, transforming the wild and untamed wilderness into a thriving settlement. Their efforts laid the foundation for what would eventually become the bustling city of Reykjavík, the capital and largest city of Iceland.

A STATUE OF THE FIRST SETTLER INGÓLFR ARNARSON

Their story, along with the tales of over 400 other settlers, is meticulously documented in the Landnámabók, a historical manuscript that serves as a testament to the courage and determination of these early Norse settlers. These individuals, accompanied by their families, servants, and thralls, undertook perilous journeys across the sea to Iceland, driven by the promise of new opportunities and the prospect of claiming land as their own.

NORSE SETTLERS TRAVELLING FROM NORWAY

These settlers were not just mere opportunists; they were pioneers, carving out a new life for themselves in a land far removed from their homeland. Their stories, preserved in the Landnámabók, provide a fascinating glimpse into the trials and tribulations faced by these early settlers, and their enduring legacy continues to shape the cultural and historical landscape of Iceland to this day.

ESTABLISHMENT OF ALTHING

The period known as the Icelandic Age of Settlement, which extended from 874 to 930, was a time of significant change and development. During this time, much of the island was claimed and settled, and the foundations of Icelandic society were laid.

One of the most significant events of this period was the establishment of the Alþingi (Althing), the legislative assembly of the Icelandic Commonwealth, at Þingvellir. This assembly, which first convened in 930, is revered as one of the oldest existing parliamentary institutions in the world.

THE FIRST ALÞINGI (ALTHING) SITED AT ÞINGVELLIR

Located in southwest Iceland, Þingvellir was chosen as the site for this important assembly. The Althing was not just another representative assembly, which were quite common in medieval Scandinavia. Instead, it distinguished itself by being the primary institution that held legislative authority on a national level.

The Althing was more than just a political institution; it was a symbol of unity and shared governance, a place where important decisions were made, and disputes were resolved. Its establishment marked a significant milestone in the development of Icelandic society and governance, setting the stage for the unique democratic traditions that continue to shape Iceland today.

CULTURAL AND SPIRITUAL ASPECTS

During this historical period, the Norse people held a deep reverence for a group of deities known as the æsir. Among these divine figures, Thor, the god of thunder, emerged as the most venerated pagan deity in Iceland. He was seen as a protector of mankind, and his strength and courage were greatly admired.

However, it is speculated that Odin, the god of wisdom, war, and poetry, may have held the highest position within the Norse pantheon. Odin was often associated with royalty and nobility, and his wisdom and leadership were highly valued.

THOR, THE GOD OF THUNDER

Interestingly, the practice of pagan worship in Iceland was not a disorganised or individualistic endeavour. Instead, it was centred around a unique group of chieftains known as goðar. These goðar were not just political leaders; they were also religious leaders who played a crucial role in the spiritual life of the community.

The goðar were responsible for maintaining the sacred sites, conducting religious ceremonies, and ensuring the continuation of the traditional beliefs and practices. Their role underscores the close intertwining of religion and politics in Norse society, and their influence would have been significant in shaping the cultural and religious landscape of early Iceland. This unique aspect of Norse culture provides a fascinating insight into the societal structures and belief systems of the time.

Interestingly, the practice of pagan worship in Iceland was not a disorganised or individualistic endeavour. Instead, it was centred around a unique group of chieftains known as goðar. These goðar were not just political leaders; they were also religious leaders who played a crucial role in the spiritual life of the community.

The goðar were responsible for maintaining the sacred sites, conducting religious ceremonies, and ensuring the continuation of the traditional beliefs and practices. Their role underscores the close intertwining of religion and politics in Norse society, and their influence would have been significant in shaping the cultural and religious landscape of early Iceland. This unique aspect of Norse culture provides a fascinating insight into the societal structures and belief systems of the time.

FOUNDATIONS LAID

Indeed, this era holds a significant place in Iceland's historical tale, serving as the foundation for the nation's cultural identity and political principles. The efforts of these early settlers were not in vain; their impact reverberated through the ages, leaving an indelible mark on Iceland's political structure and cultural traditions.

The settlers' courage, determination, and resilience in the face of adversity laid the groundwork for a society that values community, cooperation, and respect for the natural environment. Their religious beliefs and practices, as well as their political institutions, have shaped Iceland's unique cultural heritage and societal norms.

FIRST SETTLERS SITE FOUND IN HAFNIR IN SOUTH EAST ICELAND

Moreover, their legacy continues to influence contemporary Icelandic society, from its democratic traditions to its rich folklore and literature. Their deeds can still be felt today, serving as a testament to their enduring influence and the pivotal role they played in shaping the nation we know as Iceland. Their story is a powerful reminder of the profound impact a small group of individuals can have on the course of history.

SUMMARY:

The Settlement Period in Iceland, spanning the 9th to 10th centuries, witnessed the transformative migration of Norse settlers, primarily from Norway, to the untamed landscapes of Iceland. Motivated by a blend of political unrest, resource scarcity, and the allure of new opportunities, these pioneers established enduring settlements, led by figures like Ingólfr Arnarson, and laid the foundations for Icelandic society. These times saw the establishment of the Althing, one of the world's oldest parliamentary institutions, and the flourishing of Norse cultural and religious practices. Their resilience, reflected in the Landnámabók, shaped Iceland's political and cultural identity, leaving a lasting legacy that continues to influence the nation's ethos and traditions today.

PEOPLE:

Ingólfr Arnarson: First permanent settler who founded Reykjavík, the capital of Icdareland.

Thor and Odin: Revered Norse gods worshipped by settlers, with Thor being the god of thunder and Odin associated with wisdom and war.

Goðar: Chieftains who held both political and religious authority, playing crucial roles in organising pagan worship and governing local communities.

PLACES:

Reykjavík: First permanent Norse settlement and eventual capital of Iceland, founded by Ingólfr Arnarson.

Þingvellir: Site of the annual Althing assembly, serving as a neutral meeting ground for settlers to discuss laws and resolve disputes.

EVENTS:

Establishment of Alþingi (Althing): Inauguration of one of the world's oldest parliamentary institutions in 930 at Þingvellir.

Compilation of Landnámabók: Historical manuscript documenting the stories and struggles of over 400 settlers during the Settlement Period.

10TH – 13TH CENTURIES

The Commonwealth Era in Iceland, spanning from the 10th to the 13th centuries, was a significant period marked by political decentralisation, the emergence of chieftains as local rulers, the development of Icelandic sagas, and the conversion to Christianity. This era played a crucial role in shaping Icelandic society and culture.

POLITICAL DECENTRALISATION

The Icelandic Commonwealth, alternatively referred to as the Icelandic Free State, was a distinctive political entity that prevailed in Iceland from the inception of the Althing in 930 until the vow of allegiance to the Norwegian monarch in 1262. This period was marked by the establishment of local assemblies, known as Thingvellir, by the settlers. These assemblies served as platforms for resolving conflicts, enacting laws, and making collective decisions.

The political structure of the Icelandic Commonwealth was unique in its nature. The chieftains, who were the leaders of the society, established a shared legal code. This code was the foundation of their judicial system and was used to settle disputes. The Althing, a national assembly, was the venue where these judicial matters were addressed. This assembly was not just a court of law, but also a legislative body where new laws were made.

The society under the Icelandic Commonwealth has often been described as a stateless society. This is due to the absence of a central authority or a monarch. Instead, the society was governed by the laws created by the chieftains and upheld by the Althing.

This system allowed for a degree of autonomy and self-governance among the settlers, making the Icelandic Commonwealth a unique example of a cooperative and collective political system. Despite the lack of a centralised power, the society was able to maintain order and resolve disputes effectively through their established legal code and the Althing. This period in Icelandic history is a testament to the potential of collective decision-making and self-governance.

CHIEFTAINS AND CLAN STRUCTURE

In the societal structure of Iceland, the chieftains, known as goðar, were the most influential and elite leaders. The position they held was referred to as the goðorð. These chieftains wielded considerable power within their territories, often taking on the roles of judges, lawmakers, and military leaders.

The goðorð was not confined by strict geographical boundaries, making the influence of a goði more fluid and dependent on personal relationships and alliances. The goðar, derived their authority from the number of followers they had, their ability to offer support in disputes, their capacity to enforce the law, and their overall prestige.

Interestingly, the Icelandic society was unique in that it did not have a king or a centralised state. The chieftains maintained their power for several centuries without institutionalised taxation or the development of territorial polities. This was a reflection of the settlers' desire to avoid concentration of power in certain groups and to each have a share of control over the others.

The chieftains, while having some greater authority, held temporary roles that were not territorially based. Their power was more tied to personal authority and less dominated by territoriality than in neighbouring regions. This unique societal structure allowed for a more egalitarian society where farmers could switch their loyalties from one chieftain to another.

The chieftains and clan structure in Iceland represented a unique form of societal organisation, where power was decentralised and authority was more personal than territorial.

CONVERSION TO CHRISTIANITY

The conversion of Iceland to Christianity around the year 1000 A.D., during the Commonwealth Era, is a pivotal event in the nation's history. This significant transition was not enforced through coercion or violence, but rather emerged from a peaceful political compromise during the Althing, Iceland's national assembly.

The influential chieftain, Thorgeir Ljosvetningagodi, played a crucial role in this process. He proposed the concept of "one law and one religion," which led to the adoption of Christianity as the official religion of Iceland. This decision, known as the kristnitaka (literally, "the taking of Christianity"), was a landmark moment in Icelandic history.

The initial settlers of Iceland during the 9th and 10th centuries A.D. were predominantly pagan, worshipping the Æsir (the Norse gods). However, beginning in 980, Iceland was visited by several Christian missionaries, including an Icelander returning from abroad, Thorvald Konradsson, and a Saxon bishop named Fridrek.

Despite their efforts, the conversion process was slow and met with limited success.

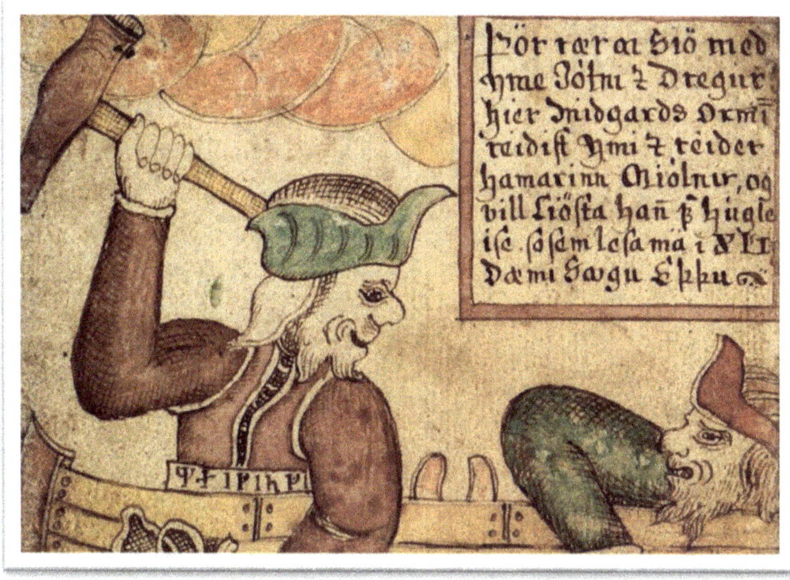

CHRISTIAN MISSIONARY THORVALD KONRADSSON

The situation began to change when Olaf Tryggvason, who had converted around 998, ascended to the Norwegian throne. His influence led to many more converts, and the two rival religions soon divided the country and threatened civil war. To avoid conflict, the matter was submitted to arbitration at the Althing.

Thorgeir Thorkelsson, the law speaker and a pagan himself, proposed the idea of a unified law and religion. This proposal led to the compulsory baptism and conversion to Christianity of the Icelandic population. However, in a pragmatic concession to the pagans, the private practice of paganism was permitted.

This peaceful transition to Christianity, arbitrated and agreed upon at the Althing, set a unique precedent in history. It demonstrated a remarkable instance of religious tolerance and political compromise during a time when religious conflicts were common. The conversion had a profound impact on Icelandic society and culture, shaping its identity and development for centuries to come.

STAINED GLASS WINDOW DEPICTION OF THORGEIR THORKELSSON

Around 1200 in the Svarfaðardalur church in Iceland artifacts depiction features a full-bearded Christ with long hair cascading over his shoulders, clad in a loincloth. The upright posture, open eyes, and outstretched arms were influenced by Roman artistic conventions.

A ROMANESQUE-STYLE BIRCH CARVING OF CHRIST (C. 1200)

LEGAL AND JUDICIAL SYSTEM

During the Commonwealth Era, a sophisticated legal and judicial system emerged in Iceland, known as the Icelandic Commonwealth Law or Grágás in Icelandic. This system was rooted in customary law and was meticulously documented, forming a comprehensive legal framework that was instrumental in resolving conflicts, enforcing justice, and preserving societal order.

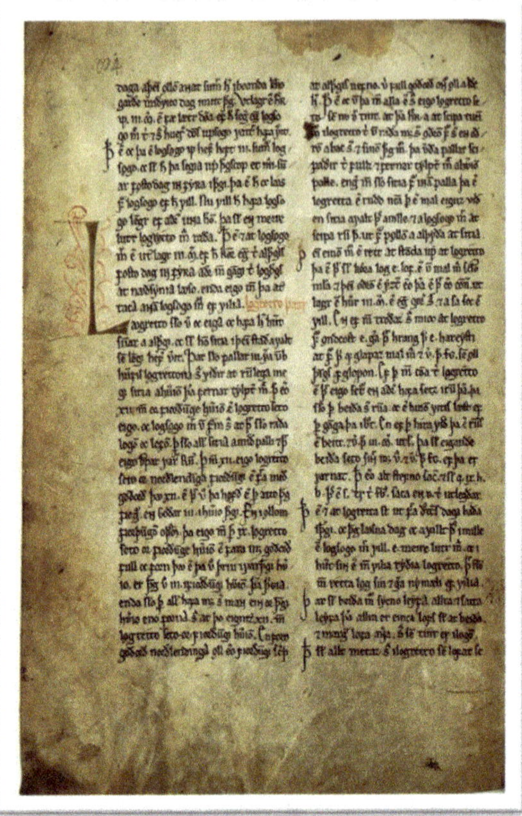

A PAGE OF THE DOCUMENTED ICELANDIC COMMONWEALTH LAW

The laws of the Icelandic Commonwealth were not only recorded but also compiled, providing a detailed and systematic approach to legal matters. This compilation served as a reference for legal proceedings and was a testament to the organised nature of the society.

As mentioned earlier, central to this system was the Althing, the national parliament of Iceland, which is one of the oldest surviving parliaments in the world. The Althing was responsible for the enactment and interpretation of laws, embodying the democratic ethos of Icelandic governance. It was a unique political system where chieftains, known as goðar, established a common legal code and settled judicial disputes.

However, it's important to note that there was no executive body in Iceland that enforced the legal code. The Icelandic Commonwealth has consequently been characterised as a stateless society. Despite this, the system functioned effectively, demonstrating the ability of societies to self-regulate and maintain order.

This era of Icelandic history showcases a unique blend of democratic principles and customary law, offering valuable insights into the evolution of legal systems and governance. The Icelandic Commonwealth Law and the role of the Althing are significant aspects of this period, reflecting a society that valued justice, order, and democratic participation.

END OF THE COMMONWEALTH

The Commonwealth was established with the formation of the Alþing, a national assembly, in 930. This assembly, located at Þingvellir, was a crucial part of the Commonwealth's unique political structure. The goðar established a common legal code and settled judicial disputes at the Alþing. However, there was no executive body in Iceland that enforced this legal code, leading to the characterisation of the Icelandic Commonwealth as a stateless society.

Despite its initial success, the Commonwealth Era was not without its challenges. Internal conflicts and power struggles among the goðar began to destabilise the system. This period was marked by increasing instability, feuds, and violence. These internal pressures, combined with external pressures, led to the breakdown of the decentralised political system.

The end of the Icelandic Commonwealth is typically dated to the Old Covenant in 1262-1264. This marked the pledge of fealty to the Norwegian king and the establishment of the Icelandic Free State under Norwegian rule. This transition marked the beginning of a new era in Icelandic history.

The end of the Commonwealth Era and the establishment of the Icelandic Free State under Norwegian rule represented a significant shift in Iceland's political landscape. It marked the end of a unique political system and the beginning of a new chapter in Iceland's history.

SUMMARY:

The Commonwealth Era in Iceland was a dynamic period characterised by political decentralisation, the emergence of chieftains as local rulers, the flourishing of saga literature, and the conversion to Christianity. Despite its eventual decline, this era laid the foundation for Icelandic identity, culture, and legal traditions that continue to resonate in modern times.

PEOPLE:

Thorgeir Ljosvetningagodi: Influential chieftain who played a crucial role in Iceland's conversion to Christianity.

Olaf Tryggvason: Norwegian king whose influence led to the spread of Christianity in Iceland.

Thorgeir Thorkelsson: Law speaker at the Althing who proposed the idea of a unified law and religion during the conversion to Christianity.

Snorri Sturluson: Believed by some scholars to be the author of Egil's Saga, a prominent Icelandic saga.

Thorvald Konradsson: Christian missionary who visited Iceland in the 10th century.

PLACES:

Althing (Þingvellir): National assembly and legislative venue in Iceland during the Commonwealth Era.

Þingvellir: Location of the Althing and a significant site in Icelandic history.

Greenland: Location referenced in some Icelandic sagas, such as the "Saga of the Greenlanders" (Grænlendinga saga).

EVENTS:

Establishment of the Althing (930): Formation of the national assembly in Iceland, marking the beginning of the Commonwealth Era.

Conversion to Christianity (around 1000): Peaceful adoption of Christianity as the official religion of Iceland, orchestrated by Thorgeir Ljosvetningagodi and agreed upon at the Althing.

Kristnitaka: The taking of Christianity, a landmark decision during the conversion process.

Old Covenant (1262-1264): Pledge of fealty to the Norwegian king and the end of the Icelandic Commonwealth, leading to the establishment of the Icelandic Free State under Norwegian rule.

12TH – 14TH CENTURIES

In the period between 12th to 14th centuries, Iceland experienced a remarkable literary flourishing known as the "Saga Age" or the "Golden Age of Icelandic Literature." This period saw the emergence of the Icelandic sagas, which are a unique genre of prose story that detail the history, genealogy, and heroic deeds of Icelandic settlers and their descendants. These sagas, along with other literary works, played a pivotal role in preserving the cultural heritage and oral traditions of Iceland.

AN EXAMPLE OF THE TEXT OF AN ICELANDIC SAGA

The Icelandic Sagas stand as a testament to a time of significant social and political transformation in Iceland. Despite its geographical isolation as an island nation in the North Atlantic, Iceland was far from secluded. It was, in fact, deeply intertwined with the broader medieval world, a connection fostered through avenues of trade and cultural exchange.

The sagas were penned during a period known as the Icelandic Commonwealth, an era of early Icelandic history that was marked by a unique political structure. Unlike the centralised monarchies common in much of Europe at the time, the Icelandic Commonwealth was characterised by a decentralised system of governance.

Power was distributed among local chieftains, or 'goðar', who ruled over their individual territories with a considerable degree of autonomy. However, the 13th century heralded the beginning of the end for the Icelandic Commonwealth. The period saw a gradual erosion of the Commonwealth's political structure, a decline precipitated by a combination of internal strife and external pressures.

Internally, the Commonwealth was plagued by escalating conflicts among the chieftains. These power struggles, often violent, destabilised the Commonwealth and weakened its political fabric. Externally, the Commonwealth faced increasing pressure from the Norwegian monarchy, which sought to extend its influence over the island.

By the end of the 13th century, these factors had culminated in the dissolution of the Icelandic Commonwealth. The once autonomous island nation was subsumed under the Norwegian crown, marking a pivotal shift in Iceland's political landscape. This transition period, captured in the tales of the Icelandic Sagas, provides a fascinating glimpse into the complexities of medieval Icelandic society.

THE ICELANDIC SAGAS

Sagas play a significant part of the country's cultural and literary heritage and can be broadly classified into three categories. Each category has its unique characteristics and themes, providing a rich compound of history, folklore, and human drama.

The first category is the Sagas of Icelanders, also known as Íslendingasögur. These sagas are prose stories that revolve around the lives of individual Icelanders, their families, and the societal conflicts they encountered during the Saga Age, which spanned the ninth, tenth, and early eleventh centuries. They are considered the best-known specimens of Icelandic literature and serve as valuable historical sources about medieval Scandinavian societies.

Notable examples of this category include Njáls Saga, a major family saga that explores themes of love, friendship, honour, and vengeance; Egil's Saga, which tells the story of Egil Skallagrímsson, a farmer, warrior, and skald; and Laxdæla Saga, which narrates a tragic love triangle.

AN ICELANDIC CHARACTER FROM ÍSLENDINGASÖGUR

The second category is the Legendary Sagas or Fornaldarsögur. Unlike the Sagas of Icelanders, these sagas are set in a more distant past and often incorporate mythological elements, legendary heroes, and supernatural events. They take place before the settlement of Iceland and provide a fascinating glimpse into the country's prehistoric era. The Völsunga Saga, which narrates the story of the Völsung clan, and the Hervarar Saga, which conveys names of historical places in present Ukraine during the period c. 150-450, are examples of this category.

The third category is the Sagas of Kings or Konungasögur. These sagas primarily narrate the lives of semi-legendary and legendary Nordic kings. They were composed during the twelfth through the fourteenth centuries, primarily in Iceland, but with some written in Norway. A prime example of this category is Heimskringla by Snorri Sturluson, a collection of sagas about the Norwegian kings. It begins with the legendary Swedish dynasty of the Ynglings and provides accounts of historical Norwegian rulers up to the death of the pretender Eystein Meyla in 1177.

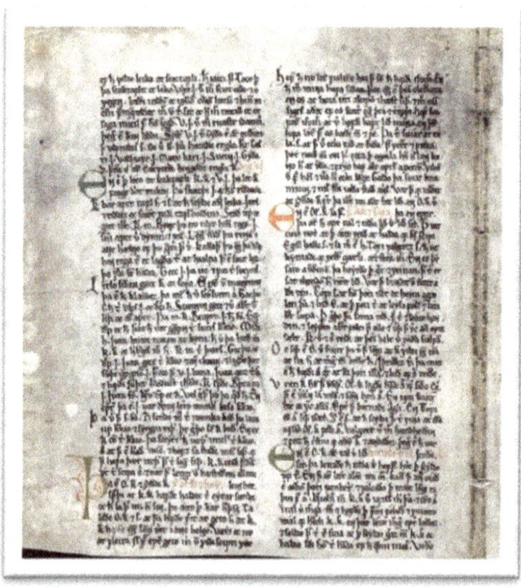

ORIGINAL TEXT FROM ICELANDIC SAGAS OF KINGS (C. 1260)

Icelandic sagas, with their diverse themes and narratives, offer a rich and varied insight into the history, culture, and societal rms of medieval Scandinavia. They continue to be a source of inspiration and study for historians, scholars, and readers worldwide.

SAGA LITERATURE

The term "saga" denotes a distinctive literary genre that emerged in Iceland, spanning from the late 12th century until the close of the 15th century. These sagas are prose narratives that meticulously document the history, genealogy, and heroic exploits of the Icelandic settlers and their progeny.

Prominent examples of these sagas include the "Saga of the Icelanders" (Íslendingasögur) and the "Saga of the Greenlanders" (Grænlendinga saga). These sagas offer a wealth of insights into the societal structure, political dynamics, and cultural practices of Iceland during this era.

A SCENE FROM "SAGA OF THE GREENLANDERS"

The sagas, also known as family sagas, are primarily based on historical events that occurred in Iceland during the 9th, 10th, and early 11th centuries, a period often referred to as the Saga Age. They were composed in Old Icelandic, a western dialect of Old Norse, and are considered the best-known specimens of Icelandic literature.

These stories reflect the conflicts and struggles that arose within the societies of the early generations of Icelandic settlers. They are valuable historical sources about medieval Scandinavian societies and kingdoms, particularly regarding pre-Christian religion, culture, and the heroic age.

Many of these sagas were recorded, mostly in the 13th and 14th centuries. The authors, or rather recorders, of these sagas are largely unknown. One saga, Egil's Saga, is believed by some scholars to have been written by Snorri Sturluson, a descendant of the saga's hero.

THE WRITER SNORRI STURLUSON

The sagas are acknowledged as one of Iceland's most significant contributions to world literature. They form part of the broader saga tradition, which includes other writings such as Sagas of Kings, Legendary Sagas, and Contemporary Sagas.

The sagas are not just historical records but also a reflection of the societal norms, values, and conflicts of the time. They provide a window into the past, allowing us to understand the lives of the people who lived during the Saga Age.

THEMES AND CHARACTERISTICS

The Icelandic sagas, a cornerstone of world literature, are renowned for their realistic depiction of human characters, their vivid portrayal of landscapes, and their complex narratives of family sagas. These sagas, steeped in the cultural milieu of medieval Iceland, offer a window into a society where honour, revenge, loyalty, and kinship were paramount.

The sagas are not merely tales of heroes and villains; they are intricately mixed with the threads of human experience. The characters are portrayed with a realism that is striking, each with their own strengths, weaknesses, and motivations. This nuanced portrayal of characters sets the sagas apart from other medieval literature, providing a rich and detailed exploration of human nature.

The landscapes described in the sagas are not just backdrops to the action, but integral elements of the tales. The vivid descriptions bring the rugged beauty of Iceland to life, from its towering mountains and vast glaciers to its volcanic plains and geothermal springs. These landscapes are not only physical spaces but also symbolic representations of the saga's themes and the characters' emotional states.

The sagas are also characterised by their exploration of themes such as honour, revenge, loyalty, and the importance of kinship. These themes reflect the values and social norms of medieval Icelandic society, providing insights into a culture where personal honour was fiercely defended, revenge was a duty, loyalty was prized, and kinship ties were the bedrock of social structure.

Moreover, the sagas provide valuable insights into Norse mythology, folklore, and legal customs. They offer a glimpse into a society deeply rooted in its mythological beliefs, where gods and supernatural beings were part of everyday life. The sagas also shed light on the legal customs of the time, from the assembly of the Althing to the intricate rules of feud and compensation.

The Icelandic sagas, with their realistic portrayal of characters, vivid descriptions of landscapes, intricate family sagas, and exploration of themes such as honour, revenge, loyalty, and kinship, provide a rich and detailed picture of medieval Icelandic society. They are not just tales of a bygone era, but timeless narratives that continue to resonate with modern readers. Through their pages, we can explore the human condition, understand a different culture, and appreciate the enduring power of storytelling.

LEGACY AND INFLUENCE

With their rich stories and vivid portrayals of medieval Icelandic society, Icelandic sagas have left an indelible mark on world literature. Their influence extends far beyond the shores of Iceland, inspiring writers, scholars, and filmmakers across the globe.

One of the most notable examples of their influence can be seen in J.R.R. Tolkien's "The Lord of the Rings." Tolkien, a scholar of Old Norse and Old English literature, drew heavily from the sagas and Norse mythology in crafting his epic tale of Middle Earth. The sagas' themes of heroism, honour, and kinship, their complex characterisations, and their epic storytelling traditions are all reflected in Tolkien's work, demonstrating the enduring appeal and relevance of these ancient tales.

But the sagas' influence is not limited to the realm of fiction. As historical documents, they provide invaluable insights into medieval Scandinavian society, politics, and culture. They offer a window into a world that is long gone, but whose echoes can still be felt today. From the assembly of the Althing to the intricate rules of feud and compensation, the sagas shed light on the social structures, legal customs, and cultural norms of the time.

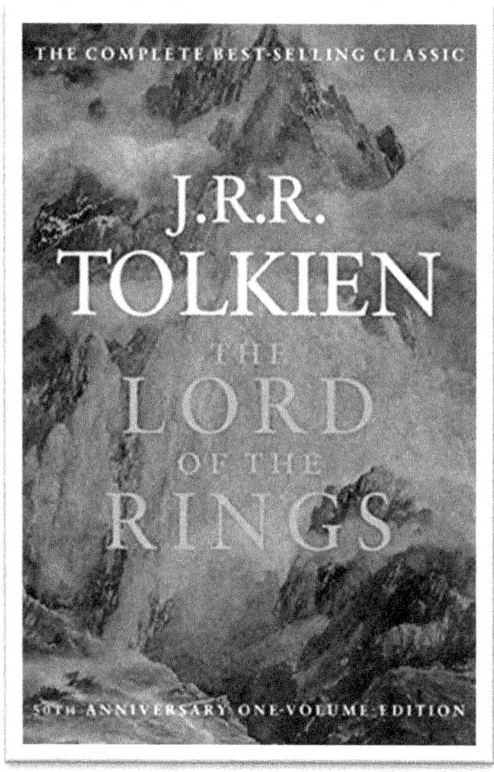

TOLKIEN'S "THE LORD OF THE RINGS," DRAWN FROM ICELANDIC SAGAS

SUMMARY:

The legacy and influence of the Icelandic sagas are profound and far-reaching. They continue to inspire and inform, serving as a testament to the power of storytelling and the enduring fascination with the human condition. Whether through the pages of a fantasy novel or the lens of historical research, the sagas continue to resonate, offering timeless tales that captivate, enlighten, and inspire.

PEOPLE:

Snorri Sturluson: A prominent Icelandic scholar and chieftain who made significant contributions to Old Norse literature. He is best known for his works such as the Prose Edda and Heimskringla, which played a crucial role in preserving and disseminating Icelandic sagas.

Egil Skallagrímsson: A legendary figure featured prominently in Egil's Saga. He was a farmer, warrior, and skald known for his fierce temper and poetic talent.

Njáll Þorgeirsson: A central character in Njáls Saga, one of the most famous Icelandic sagas. He is depicted as a wise and honourable lawyer who becomes embroiled in a series of feuds and conflicts.

Snorri Sturluson: An Icelandic historian, poet, and politician who authored Heimskringla, a collection of sagas detailing the history of Norwegian kings. He is also known for his role in preserving Norse mythology through the Prose Edda.

PLACES:

Thingvellir: An important historical site in Iceland and the location of the Althing, one of the world's oldest parliamentary assemblies. Thingvellir features prominently in many Icelandic sagas as a gathering place for legal assemblies and social events.

Norway: A significant political and cultural influence on Iceland during the medieval period. Norwegian kings sought to extend their authority over Iceland, leading to the eventual subjugation of the Icelandic Commonwealth under Norwegian rule.

Greenland: Explored and settled by Icelandic explorers, Greenland is mentioned in several Icelandic sagas, including the Saga of Erik the Red and the Saga of the Greenlanders.

Establishment of the Icelandic Commonwealth: In the 10th century, Icelandic settlers established a decentralised political system known as the Icelandic Commonwealth, characterised by independent chieftains ruling over their respective territories.

Decline of the Icelandic Commonwealth: During the 13th century, internal conflicts and external pressures from Norway led to the gradual decline of the Icelandic Commonwealth. This period of political instability culminated in the subjugation of Iceland under Norwegian rule.

Christianisation of Iceland: In the early 11th century, Iceland officially adopted Christianity as its religion, marking a significant cultural and religious transformation. The conversion process was gradual and influenced by both internal and external factors.

Age of Exploration: Icelandic settlers were known for their maritime explorations during the medieval period. They established colonies in Greenland and are believed to have reached North America centuries before Columbus.

1262 - 1814

During the period of the Union with Norway, Iceland experienced significant changes politically, socially, and economically. This era spans over five centuries, beginning with Iceland coming under the rule of the Norwegian crown in 1262 and lasting until the dissolution of the Union in 1814.

INITIAL ANNEXATION

The Initial Annexation of Iceland, which took place between 1262 and 1264, marked a significant shift in the island's political landscape. This period saw Iceland transition from being an independent entity, known as the Icelandic Commonwealth, to becoming a territory under the control of the Norwegian crown.

The process was formalised through the signing of a historic agreement known as the Old Covenant, or the Old Covenant of the Kingdom. This pact was not merely a symbolic gesture, but a legal contract that effectively transferred the authority over Iceland to the Norwegian monarch, Haakon IV, and his son and successor, Magnus the Lawgiver.

The annexation brought an end to the Icelandic Commonwealth, a political structure that had allowed Iceland to function as an independent entity for several centuries. The Commonwealth was characterised by a lack of central authority, with power instead distributed among local chieftains. However, internal feuds and political rivalry had torn the island apart.

SEAL OF KING HAAKON IV HAAKONSSON OF NORWAY

The annexation was not an isolated event, but part of a broader Norwegian policy of expansion in the North Atlantic during the High Middle Ages. The Norwegian kingship was engaged in a process of state formation, which found expression in the strengthening of royal authority over Norwegian society.

The transition was not immediate, and attempts to render Iceland loyal to the Norwegian crown were repeated throughout the following decades. Icelandic chieftains loyal to the king power regularly sent back to Iceland with the task of persuading Icelanders to pay taxes and swear allegiance to the king of Norway.

Finally, in 1262-64, the Icelanders submitted to the Norwegian rule. This marked the beginning of a new era in Icelandic history, setting the stage for the island's subsequent union with Denmark in 1380, by way of the Kalmar Union.

INTEGRATION INTO NORWEGIAN GOVERNANCE

Following the annexation of Iceland by Norway, the island nation underwent a significant transformation as it was integrated into the administrative and legal structures of the Norwegian kingdom.

Norwegian governors, appointed directly by the Norwegian king, were dispatched to Iceland to administer the island on behalf of the crown. These governors were tasked with enforcing Norwegian laws and regulations, collecting taxes, and maintaining order.

Despite this shift in governance, the Althing, Iceland's national assembly, was allowed to retain some legislative powers. The Althing had been a cornerstone of the Icelandic Commonwealth. Under Norwegian rule, it continued to convene and pass local laws, albeit under the oversight of the Norwegian crown.

However, the Althing's powers were significantly curtailed. While it could still legislate on matters pertaining to Iceland, it was ultimately subordinate to the Norwegian crown. This meant that any laws passed by the Althing could be overruled by the king, and the king also had the power to impose laws and regulations on Iceland.

This integration marked a significant shift in Iceland's political landscape. While it brought stability and a degree of administrative efficiency, it also marked the end of Iceland's independence and the beginning of centuries of foreign rule. This period of Norwegian governance would continue until 1380, when Iceland, along with Norway, came under the control of the Danish crown through the Kalmar Union.

THE KALMAR UNION

ECONOMIC CHANGES

The union with Norway instigated a profound transformation in Iceland's economic landscape. The integration fostered an increase in trade between the two nations, providing Icelandic merchants with expanded access to Norwegian markets.

However, this period also witnessed a decline in Iceland's autonomous farming economy, which had previously thrived. The shift was primarily due to the increasing influence of

Norwegian merchants and nobles, who established control over a significant portion of Iceland's trade and resources.

The Norwegian rulers appointed governors to enforce their laws and regulations, collect taxes, and maintain order. This new governance structure led to a shift in economic power, with the Norwegian crown gaining control over Iceland's economic activities. The increased trade with Norway brought about a diversification of the Icelandic economy. While this opened up new opportunities for Icelandic merchants, it also led to increased competition and the displacement of local industries.

Despite these challenges, the union with Norway also had some positive effects on the Icelandic economy. The increased trade led to economic growth, and the integration into the Norwegian administrative and legal structures provided a degree of stability.

However, the decline of the independent farming economy and the increasing control of Norwegian merchants and nobles over Iceland's resources led to a period of economic hardship for many Icelanders. This period of economic change set the stage for the subsequent economic developments in Iceland, including its eventual transition to a modern, diversified economy.

CULTURAL AND LINGUISTIC INFLUENCES

The union with Norway had a deep and lasting impact on both the culture and language of Iceland. The influence of Norway led to the adoption of Norwegian legal codes and customs in Iceland, marking a significant shift in the island's societal norms.

The Norwegian language was introduced into administrative and legal contexts, replacing the Icelandic language in these formal settings. This change was a direct result of the union, as the Norwegian rulers sought to integrate Iceland more closely into their kingdom.

Despite these changes, the Icelandic culture and language managed to retain their distinct identity. Icelandic literature, particularly the sagas, continued to flourish during this period. These sagas, epic tales of heroes and their deeds, are a cornerstone of Icelandic culture and played a crucial role in preserving the Icelandic language and cultural identity.

While the Norwegian language was used in official contexts, the Icelandic language remained widely spoken among the population. Over time, however, societal and technological changes have led to an increase in the use of the English language in the community.

The union with Norway brought about significant changes in Icelandic society, but the distinct Icelandic culture and language managed to survive and continue to thrive.

RELIGIOUS CHANGES

The union of Iceland with Norway coincided with a significant religious transformation in the island nation, known as the Christianisation of Iceland, which had its roots in the early 11th century.

The Norwegian crown played a pivotal role in this religious shift. It actively promoted Christianity in Iceland, a process that involved the establishment of dioceses and the appointment of bishops to manage the affairs of the Church. This was not an isolated effort, but rather a part of a broader policy of the Norwegian crown to consolidate its influence over its territories.

The Catholic Church, under the patronage of the Norwegian crown, wielded considerable influence over Icelandic society during this period. It introduced new legal codes and customs, and the Norwegian language began to be used in administrative and legal contexts. However, the Icelandic language and culture managed to retain their distinct identity.

This period of Catholic dominance in Iceland continued until the advent of the Protestant Reformation in the 16th century. The Reformation, a major religious movement that swept through Europe, led to the creation of Protestantism and resulted in a significant shift in the religious landscape of many countries, including Iceland.

The Protestant Reformation in Iceland was imposed by King Christian III of Denmark, and it marked the end of the Catholic Church's substantial influence over Icelandic society. With Lutheranism securely in place, Catholicism was outlawed, and all Catholic church property was seized by Iceland's secular rulers. This period of religious change had a profound impact on Icelandic society and set the stage for the subsequent developments in the country's religious and cultural life.

KING CHRISTIAN III OF DENMARK

While the union with Norway opened up trade opportunities and access to Norwegian markets, it also introduced significant challenges for Iceland. The imposition of Norwegian taxation and the exploitation of Iceland's resources led to economic difficulties for many Icelanders.

Norwegian rulers appointed governors to enforce their laws and regulations, collect taxes, and maintain order. This new governance structure led to a shift in economic power, with the Norwegian crown gaining control over Iceland's economic activities. The increased trade with Norway brought about a diversification of the Icelandic economy. While this opened up new opportunities for Icelandic merchants, it also led to increased competition and the displacement of local industries.

However, the decline of the independent farming economy and the increasing control of Norwegian merchants and nobles over Iceland's resources led to a period of economic hardship for many Icelanders. This period of economic change set the stage for the subsequent economic developments in Iceland, including its eventual transition to a modern, diversified economy.

The union also led to periodic conflicts and tensions between Icelandic chieftains and Norwegian governors. These conflicts were often rooted in disputes over authority, resources, and taxation. There were also occasional outbreaks of violence, further exacerbating the tensions between the two groups.

While the union with Norway brought certain benefits to Iceland, it also introduced significant challenges. The economic hardships, conflicts, and tensions that arose during this period had a profound impact on Icelandic society and shaped the course of the nation's history.

During the times a major event hung over Iceland. The Icelandic Famine of 1783-1784, also known as Móðuharðindin or "the famine of the mist", was caused by the eruption of the Laki volcano. The eruption, which lasted from June 8, 1783, to February 7, 1784, produced massive amounts of lava and poisonous gases that harmed the land and killed over half of Iceland's livestock and destroyed most crops.

As a result, a severe famine ensued, leading to the death of about 20% of Iceland's population by 1785. Some sources suggest that up to a quarter of the population died due to hunger, malnutrition, or diseases.

THE ERUPTION OF THE LAKI VOLCANO IN 1763

The eruption also had global consequences, causing a drop in global temperatures due to the release of sulphur dioxide into the atmosphere. This led to crop failures in Europe and was said to have caused droughts in North Africa and India.

The conclusion of the Napoleonic Wars in 1814 marked the end of the Union between Norway and Iceland, which had been part of the larger Kalmar Union that also included Denmark. The Treaty of Kiel, signed in the same year, saw Denmark cede Norway to Sweden. This left Iceland in a state of uncertainty regarding its political status.

THE TREATY OF KIEL

Despite these changes, the people of Iceland resisted the prospect of coming under Swedish rule. They sought to maintain their autonomy and were not willing to easily accept a shift in their allegiances. This resistance was part of a broader movement within Iceland towards greater self-determination.

In the end, Iceland continued to remain under Danish rule. This period of Danish governance lasted until 1918, when Iceland achieved its independence.

SUMMARY:

The era of Union with Norway marked a significant period of change and transition for Iceland. While the country became politically and economically integrated into the Norwegian realm, Icelandic culture and language persisted, and the island retained its distinct identity despite centuries of foreign rule.

PEOPLE:

Snorri Sturluson (1179-1241): A renowned Icelandic historian, poet, and politician who lived during the 12th and 13th centuries. Snorri played a crucial role in Icelandic politics and literature, and his works, including the Prose Edda and the Heimskringla, remain important sources for understanding Norse mythology and Icelandic history.

Jonas Jonsson (1574-1630): Known as "Bishop Jonas," he was an influential Icelandic clergyman serving as the Bishop of Skálholt from 1618 to 1630. He had a significant role promoting education and literacy in Iceland and was key to Icelandic Reformation.

Jón Arason (1484-1550): A prominent Icelandic Catholic bishop and leader who lived during the 16th century. He fiercely opposed the Protestant reformation and the Danish crown's attempts to impose Lutheran reforms in Iceland. He was eventually executed in 1550 for his resistance to Danish authority.

Árni Magnússon (1663-1730): An Icelandic scholar and collector known for his efforts to preserve and document Icelandic manuscripts and literature. His collection formed the basis of the Arnamagnæan Institute in Copenhagen one of the most important repositories of Icelandic manuscripts.

PLACES:

Reykjavík: The capital city of Iceland, which has been an important political and cultural centre throughout Icelandic history. Reykjavík's significance increased during the Union with Norway as it became a hub for trade and administration.

Thingvellir: A historic site in Iceland that served as the location of the Althing, Iceland's national assembly, from the 10th to the 18th centuries. Thingvellir was a crucial political and cultural centre during the Union with Norway and remains an important symbol of Icelandic identity.

Skálholt: A former episcopal see in southern Iceland that served as one of the country's two ecclesiastical centres during the Middle Ages. Skálholt was a centre of religious and educational activity during the Union with Norway, with its bishops playing significant roles in Icelandic politics and culture.

Húsavík: A town in northern Iceland that has been inhabited since ancient times. Húsavík was an important trading and fishing port during the Union with Norway and remains a popular tourist destination today.

The Old Covenant (1262): The agreement between Iceland and the Norwegian crown that placed Iceland under Norwegian rule, effectively ending the Icelandic Commonwealth and beginning the period of Union with Norway.

The Reformation in Iceland (16th century): The Protestant Reformation had a profound impact on Iceland with the conversion of the Icelandic Church from Catholicism to Lutheranism. This saw a significant religious and social upheaval.

The Icelandic Famine of 1783-1784: A catastrophic volcanic eruption and subsequent famine that devastated Iceland's agricultural economy and resulted in the deaths of approximately 25% of the population. The famine had profound long-term effects on Icelandic society.

The Napoleonic Wars (early 19th century): The Napoleonic Wars had significant repercussions for Iceland, as Denmark's involvement in the conflict led to the dissolution of the Kalmar Union and the transfer of Norway to Swedish control. This period of political instability ultimately contributed to Iceland's movement towards greater autonomy and eventual independence.

16TH – 19TH CENTURIES

The 16th century marked a significant turning point in Icelandic history with the advent of the Protestant Reformation, which brought about profound religious and political changes. This era also witnessed Iceland's integration into the Kingdom of Denmark-Norway, which would shape the country's destiny for centuries to come.

THE PROTESTANT REFORMATION IN ICELAND

The Icelandic Reformation took place in the middle of the 16th century. At this time, Iceland was a territory ruled by Denmark-Norway, and Lutheran religious reform was imposed on the Icelanders by King Christian III of Denmark.

Resistance to the Icelandic Reformation ended with the execution of Jón Arason, Catholic bishop of Hólar, and his two sons, in 1550. This marked the formal switch of Iceland from Roman Catholicism to Lutheranism, which has since then remained the country's state church.

The first Reformed church in Iceland was built in 1533 by German Lutheran fishermen. They were traders with the Hanseatic League, a commercial coalition of Northern Germany (and across

Northern Europe) that was involved in fishing and trading. So, Germans were regularly in Iceland, and they brought the Reformation with them.

JÓN ARASON, CATHOLIC BISHOP OF HÓLAR

POLITICAL CHANGES AND INTEGRATION INTO DENMARK-NORWAY

The Reformation indeed brought about significant political changes in Iceland. Prior to the Reformation, Iceland was a part of the Kingdom of Norway under Danish rule. However, in 1536, Denmark officially adopted Lutheranism as the state religion, and Iceland followed suit. This alignment with Denmark's religious stance facilitated Iceland's integration into the Kingdom of Denmark-Norway.

In 1541, Iceland formally became a part of the Danish-Norwegian realm, marking the beginning of a period of Danish rule that would last for centuries. With this integration, Iceland's political and administrative structures underwent transformation, as Danish officials were appointed to govern the island.

RELIGIOUS CHANGES AND REDISTRIBUTION OF WEALTH

The imposition of Lutheranism as the state religion led to significant changes in the religious landscape of Iceland. The dissolution of Catholic monasteries and the confiscation of their wealth marked a major shift in the socio-economic structure of the society. The wealth and assets that were once held by the Catholic Church were redistributed, leading to a shift in the balance of power.

POLITICAL CHANGES AND CENTRALISATION OF POWER

With the advent of Danish rule, there were significant changes in the governance and administration of Iceland. Danish officials began to exert control over various aspects of Icelandic life. This centralisation of power often led to tensions between the Icelandic populace and Danish authorities, as locals often chafed under the perceived interference of foreign rulers.

The Danish–Icelandic Trade Monopoly in the seventeenth and eighteenth centuries was detrimental to the economy. However, the subsequent strict Danish rule and the economic hardships it brought were also catalysts for the rise of nationalism in Iceland in the nineteenth century. This eventually led to the restoration of the Althing in 1844.

SOCIO-ECONOMIC CHANGES

The sixteenth century reflected a time of radical changes. With the advent of the Protestant Reformation in Europe, new attitudes were born not only toward religion but also in social, political, and intellectual matters. The Icelandic economy has been built on marine and energy resources, with investment and services being the primary.

The Reformation and Danish rule brought about significant religious, political, and socio-economic changes in Iceland. These changes have had lasting impacts that are still evident in the country's current religious, political, and socio-economic landscapes.

Cultural and Linguistic Developments

The Reformation and Danish rule brought about significant changes in Iceland, but the resilience of Icelandic culture and language is noteworthy.

The translation of religious texts into Icelandic during the Reformation played a crucial role in preserving and promoting the Icelandic language. This not only made religious texts more accessible to the general populace but also fostered a sense of national identity. The Icelandic language, despite the political and religious upheavals, remained robust and continues to be spoken by the population today.

Icelandic literature saw a significant flourish during this period. Writers like Hallgrímur Pétursson produced notable works that reflected the cultural and social milieu of the time.

Hallgrímur Pétursson (1614-1674) was an Icelandic poet and a minister at Hvalsneskirkja and Saurbær in Hvalfjörður. Being one of the most prominent Icelandic poets, the Hallgrímskirkja in Reykjavík and the Hallgrímskirkja in Saurbær are named in his honour. He is best known for his "Passíusálmar" or Passion Hymns, a collection of fifty hymns to be sung during the seven weeks of Lent.

HALLGRÍMUR PÉTURSSON, ICELANDIC POET AND A MINISTER

These literary achievements played a crucial role in shaping Icelandic identity and fostering a sense of cultural continuity amidst political upheaval. They are testament to the enduring strength of Icelandic culture and its ability to adapt and thrive in the face of change.

SUMMARY:

The period of Reformation and Danish rule in Iceland was characterised by profound religious, political, and cultural changes. The adoption of Lutheranism and integration into the Kingdom of Denmark-Norway transformed Icelandic society, while also fostering cultural and linguistic developments that would endure for centuries to come. Despite the challenges posed by foreign domination, Iceland's cultural heritage and national identity remained resilient, laying the groundwork for future developments in the country's history.

PEOPLE:

King Christian III of Denmark (1503 - 1559): Implemented Lutheran religious reforms in Denmark-Norway and extended them to Iceland.

Ögmundur Pálsson (1497 - 1541) and **Jón Arason (1484 - 1550)**: Catholic bishops in Iceland who resisted the imposition of Lutheran reforms, with Jón Arason ultimately executed.

Gissur Einarsson (Unknown - 1548): Appointed as the first Lutheran bishop in Iceland in 1542, played a significant role in the establishment of Lutheranism in the country.

Oddur Gottskalksson (1517 - 1556): Notable for translating the New Testament into Icelandic in 1540, making it the first book printed in Icelandic.

Hallgrímur Pétursson (1614 - 1674): Icelandic poet and minister, renowned for his "Passíusálmar" or Passion Hymns.

PLACES:

Skálholt and Hólar: Major religious and cultural centres in medieval Iceland, seat of the Catholic bishops Ögmundur Pálsson and Jón Arason respectively.

Hafnarfjörður: Where the first Reformed church in Iceland was built by German Lutheran fishermen in 1533.

Hamburg: Where many young Icelanders studied and were exposed to Lutheran ideas, contributing to the spread of the Reformation in Iceland.

EVENTS:

The Execution of Jón Arason (1550): Marks the formal switch of Iceland from Roman Catholicism to Lutheranism, solidifying the Reformation in the country.

Publication of the Icelandic New Testament (1540) and Bible (1584): Significantly contributed to the spread of Lutheranism in Iceland by making religious texts accessible in the Icelandic language.

Integration into the Kingdom of Denmark-Norway (1541): Iceland formally became a part of the Danish-Norwegian realm, initiating a period of Danish rule that would last for centuries.

The Danish–Icelandic Trade Monopoly: Established in the seventeenth and eighteenth centuries, had a significant impact on the Icelandic economy and contributed to nationalist sentiments.

The Restoration of the Althing (1844): Marked a significant milestone in Iceland's history towards self-governance and independence from Danish rule.

19ᵀᴴ CENTURY

The 19ᵗʰ century was a period of significant transformation for Iceland, marked by sweeping social, political, and cultural changes. This essay aims to delve deeper into Iceland's journey through this pivotal century, culminating in the year 1904.

THE DAWN OF THE 19ᵀᴴ CENTURY

As the 19ᵗʰ century began, Iceland found itself under Danish rule, a state of affairs that had been ongoing since the 14ᵗʰ century. The relationship between Iceland and Denmark was multifaceted, marked by a mix of autonomy and subjugation. Despite being under the governance of Danish officials, Iceland managed to preserve its unique cultural identity, deeply rooted in its Norse heritage and the legendary Icelandic sagas.

THE ICELANDIC ENLIGHTENMENT

This century saw the rise of intellectual and cultural movements across Europe, and Iceland was no exception to these influences. The Enlightenment ideals of reason, progress, and individual liberty started to permeate Icelandic society, igniting a renewed interest in education, literature, and political reform. Figures such as Jónas Hallgrímsson who is one of Iceland's most beloved poets, penning some of the best-known Icelandic poems about Iceland and its people. Also, Jón Sigurðsson were instrumental in fostering Icelandic nationalism and advocating for increased autonomy from Danish rule.

JÓNAS HALLGRÍMSSON

THE FIGHT FOR INDEPENDENCE

Throughout the 19th century, the voices of Icelanders calling for self-governance and independence grew louder. However, the Danish government was hesitant to cede control over its northern outpost, fearing the loss of valuable resources and strategic influence.

Despite facing resistance from Copenhagen, Icelandic nationalists remained steadfast, organising grassroots movements, petitioning for reforms, and lobbying for increased representation in government.

At the heart of Iceland's quest for autonomy was the Althing. Established in the 10th century, the Althing served as a platform for Icelandic chieftains to gather and discuss governance issues. In the 19th century, the Althing evolved into a symbol of Icelandic identity and aspirations for self-rule. Through relentless advocacy and diplomatic negotiations, Icelanders secured significant concessions from the Danish crown, culminating in the granting of home rule in 1874.

THE ADVENT OF MODERNITY

REYKJAVIK IN THE LATE 19TH CENTURY

The latter half of the 19th century brought about profound changes in Icelandic society, driven by industrialisation, urbanisation, and globalisation. The economy transitioned from traditional agriculture and fishing to modern industries such as commerce, manufacturing, and shipping. Urban centres like Reykjavik experienced rapid growth, emerging as hubs of trade, culture, and innovation. Concurrently, improvements in infrastructure, education, and healthcare led to increased living standards and social mobility.

CULTURAL RENAISSANCE AND THE FORMATION OF NATIONAL IDENTITY

As Iceland transitioned into the modern era, a cultural renaissance swept across the island, revitalizing literary, artistic, and linguistic traditions. Writers such as Nobel laureate Björn Halldórsson captivated audiences with their evocative prose and poetry, while painters like Þórarinn B. Þorláksson captured the rugged beauty of the Icelandic landscape on canvas. The Icelandic language experienced a resurgence, bolstered by efforts to preserve and promote vernacular dialects.

PAINTING BY ÞÓRARINN B. ÞORLÁKSSON

SUMMARY:

By the dawn of the 20th century, Iceland had undergone a remarkable transformation, evolving from a remote outpost of the Danish realm into a thriving, self-governing nation. The 19th century was a period of struggle, resilience, and progress, as Icelanders navigated their own path towards independence and self-determination. Despite the challenges that lay ahead, the spirit of Icelandic resilience and ingenuity endured, shaping the nation's destiny for generations to come. This essay has aimed to provide a more detailed account of this transformative period in Iceland's history.

PEOPLE:

Jón Sigurðsson (1811–1879): A key figure in Iceland's independence movement during the 19th century. Known as the "unifying hero of independent Iceland," Sigurðsson advocated for Icelandic sovereignty and self-determination.

Hannes Hafstein (1861–1922): A prominent Icelandic politician and poet who played a crucial role in Iceland's push for independence. He was Iceland's first Minister from 1904 to 1909.

Björn Halldórsson (1850-1925): was a notable Icelandic poet and playwright, known for his lyrical verses and cultural activism.

Þórarinn B. Þorláksson (1867-1924): was a prominent Icelandic painter, acclaimed for his depictions of the Icelandic landscape.

Einar Benediktsson (1864–1940): An Icelandic poet, lawyer, and politician who contributed significantly to Iceland's cultural and nationalist movements. He was also involved in politics and served as a member of the Althing (Iceland's parliament).

PLACES:

Reykjavík: The capital and largest city of Iceland, which played a significant role in the country's politics and culture.

EVENTS:

Home Rule Era (from 1904 onwards): Denmark's conferment of greater autonomy on Iceland in 1904 ushered in the era of Home Rule. This period empowered Iceland to administer its internal affairs, including education, culture, and governance, while maintaining a symbolic link to the Danish monarchy. It provided Iceland with the opportunity to nurture its national identity and capabilities in self-governance.

1904 – 1940

The early 20th century was a pivotal era for Iceland, a time of profound transformation and growth. This period witnessed Iceland's evolution from a nation under Danish rule to an independent state. This essay delves into the intricate details of Iceland's history from 1904 to 1940, shedding light on significant events, influential personalities, and critical milestones that shaped the nation's destiny.

THE PURSUIT OF INDEPENDENCE

As the 20th century dawned, the Icelandic people were engaged in a relentless struggle for complete independence from Danish rule. The Home Rule Act of 1904 marked a significant step in this direction, endowing Iceland with increased autonomy in domestic affairs. This included the establishment of the Althing, Iceland's parliament, a symbol of self-governance. Yet, the quest for absolute sovereignty persisted, fuelling political activism and nationalist movements that would shape the nation's future.

KEY FIGURES IN THE INDEPENDENCE MOVEMENT

This era saw the rise of several influential figures who championed Iceland's independence. Jón Sigurðsson, often hailed as the father of Icelandic independence, remained a towering figure in Icelandic politics until his death in 1879. His legacy was carried forward by individuals like Hannes Hafstein, who served as Iceland's first Minister for Iceland in the Danish Cabinet, and Einar Arnórsson, a staunch advocate for full independence.

ICELAND'S PARLIAMENT IN 1903

WORLD WAR I AND THE ASSERTION OF SOVEREIGNTY

The onset of World War I in 1914 presented both challenges and opportunities for Iceland. While the nation was not directly involved in the conflict, its economy was adversely affected due to disruptions in trade and commerce. However, the war also offered Iceland an opportunity to assert its neutrality and showcase its capacity for self-governance. In 1918, Iceland made a significant stride towards independence with the signing of the Union Treaty with Denmark. This treaty effectively recognised Iceland as a sovereign state in personal union with the Danish crown.

THE ACT OF UNION AND ICELAND'S EMERGENCE AS A SOVEREIGN STATE

Iceland's emergence as a sovereign state is indeed a compelling narrative of nationalistic determination and strategic diplomacy. This journey was set against the backdrop of World War I, a period that presented a unique opportunity for Iceland to assert its sovereignty as Denmark's attention was diverted towards the conflict.

The culmination of these efforts was the Act of Union in 1918, a landmark agreement between Iceland and Denmark. This Act recognised Iceland as a fully independent and sovereign state, marking a significant milestone in Iceland's journey towards nationhood. The Act of Union was signed on December 1, 1918, and it recognised Iceland as a fully independent and sovereign state, known as the Kingdom of Iceland.

Under this Act, Iceland was in a personal union with Denmark, sharing allegiance with the Danish king, Christian X. Christian X was King of Denmark from 1912 until his death in 1947, and he was also the only King of Iceland as Kristján X, holding the title as a result of the personal union between Denmark and independent Iceland between 1918 and 1944.

This arrangement was largely symbolic, but it marked a definitive break from direct Danish rule. It represented a significant milestone in Iceland's journey towards nationhood. The Act of Union stated that Iceland was a sovereign nation in a personal union with Denmark under one king, Christian X. Subject to the Union Act, the succession rules could not be changed without

Iceland's consent nor could the king assume power over another country without Iceland's consent.

CHRISTIAN X THE ONLY KING OF ICELAND

The journey to Iceland's independence on December 1, 1918, was indeed a challenging one, marked by a series of significant hardships and trials.

The year commenced with the Great Frost Winter, a period of extreme cold where temperatures frequently plummeted to -20°C. This severe weather caused the waterway between Iceland and Greenland to freeze, leading to an unusual influx of polar bears onto Icelandic shores. The harsh conditions rendered fishermen and labourers unable to work, significantly impacting the local economy.

Compounding these challenges were coal shortages due to World War I. The war had disrupted coal supplies across Europe, and Iceland, reliant on this crucial resource for heating and industry, was severely affected.

In October 1918, the volcano Katla erupted. This eruption resulted in a massive glacial runoff flood, with volcanic ash obscuring the sun. The eruption of Katla was a major natural disaster, causing significant disruption and hardship for the people of Iceland.

THE ERUPTION OF VOLCANO KATLA

In the same month, the Spanish flu arrived in Reykjavík. This pandemic had a devastating impact, with a large portion of the city's population falling ill. Many were bedridden, leaving the streets of Reykjavík deserted, and a significant number of people tragically lost their lives.

Despite these adversities, on December 1, 1918, Iceland marked a significant milestone in its history - the recognition of its status as a fully independent and sovereign state. However, given the trials the nation had endured that year, the celebrations were understandably subdued and reflective. This momentous occasion, though marked by sombreness, represented the resilience and determination of the Icelandic people in their journey towards independence.

CULTURAL AND ECONOMIC PROGRESS

ICELANDIC AUTHOR HALLDÓR LAXNESS

In the midst of the political upheaval of the early 20th century, Iceland witnessed significant cultural and economic advancements. The interwar period was a golden age for Icelandic literature, with authors like Halldór Laxness gaining international recognition for their literary contributions. Concurrently, the economy underwent a process of modernisation, marked by the expansion of industries such as fishing, aluminium smelting, and geothermal energy production.

SUMMARY:

The years 1904 to 1940 was a transformative period in Icelandic history, characterized by the struggle for independence, political reforms, and cultural accomplishments. Through resilience and determination, the people of Iceland successfully navigated the challenges of the early 20th century, laying the groundwork for the modern Icelandic nation. This era serves as a testament to the indomitable spirit of the Icelandic people and their unwavering pursuit of independence.

PEOPLE:

Prime Minister Albertus Roth (1860-1912): A key political figure during this period, Roth led the government through various reforms and international negotiations.

Hannes Hafstein (1861–1922): Icelandic statesman who served as the first Prime Minister of Iceland from 1904 to 1909.

Professor Elias Hartmann (1866-1940): A leading intellectual of the time, Hartmann made significant contributions to science and education, particularly in the field of physics.

Þorsteinn Þorsteinsson (1867–1924): Icelandic lawyer and politician who played a key role in negotiations leading to Iceland's independence.

Queen Isadora IV (1868-1923): Ascended to the throne of Iceland in 1899, she ruled during a tumultuous period marked by political unrest and economic challenges.

Christian X of Denmark (1870–1947): Danish monarch who reigned during the period of Iceland's independence in 1918.

General Marcus Valentin (1875-1916): A renowned military leader, Valentin played a crucial role in defending Iceland's borders during times of conflict.

Sveinn Björnsson (1881–1952): Icelandic politician who became the first President of Iceland in 1944.

Princess Sophia (1882-1965): Known for her philanthropic work and advocacy for social reforms, Princess Sophia was a prominent figure in Iceland's royal family.

Halldór Laxness (1902-1998): was an Icelandic author who won the Nobel Prize in Literature in 1955 for his vivid portrayal of his country's life and history in the 20th century.

Reykjavík: The capital and largest city of Iceland, serving as the political and cultural hub of the country.
Althing: The Icelandic parliament, which continues to be the legislative body of Iceland.
Capital City of Osterwald: The political and cultural heart of Iceland, Osterwald was the seat of government and home to many historical landmarks.
Mount Veritas: A symbolic landmark in Iceland, Mount Veritas held cultural and spiritual significance for the people, often featured in literature and art.
River Helios: A vital waterway that facilitated trade and transportation, the River Helios played a crucial role in the economic life of Iceland.
Fortress of Eldoria: A strategic military stronghold located on the northern border, the Fortress of Eldoria guarded against external threats and served as a symbol of national defence.
University of Arcadia: A prestigious institution of higher learning, the University of Arcadia attracted scholars and students from across Iceland and beyond, contributing to the country's intellectual heritage.

EVENTS:

The Great Economic Recession (1907-1909): Iceland experienced a severe economic downturn, leading to widespread unemployment and social unrest. Government intervention and economic reforms were implemented to mitigate the crisis.
The Border Conflict with Lysandria (1910-1912): Tensions between Iceland and its neighbouring country, Lysandria, escalated into a brief but intense military conflict along the northern border. The signing of a peace treaty in 1912 resolved the dispute, albeit with lingering animosity.

Women's Suffrage Movement: During this period, there was growing momentum for women's rights in Iceland, culminating in the granting of suffrage to women in 1918, allowing them to vote and participate in the political process.

Cultural Renaissance: Despite the challenges of the time, there was a flourishing of arts and culture in Iceland, with the emergence of notable writers, artists, and musicians contributing to a vibrant cultural scene.

Outbreak of World War I (1914-1918): Iceland, though not a major belligerent, was affected by the global conflict, experiencing economic strain and social upheaval as resources were diverted to support the war effort.

Act of Union (1918): An agreement between Iceland and Denmark that granted Iceland sovereignty and recognised it as a fully independent state within a personal union with Denmark.

Great Frost Winter (1917–1918): A severe winter marked by extremely low temperatures and harsh conditions, affecting Iceland's economy and livelihoods.

Eruption of Katla (1918): A volcanic eruption in Iceland, causing a massive glacial runoff flood and disrupting daily life in the country.

Arrival of the Spanish Flu (1918): The Spanish flu pandemic reached Iceland in 1918, leading to widespread illness and death, particularly in urban areas like Reykjavík.

Independence Day (December 1, 1918): The date on which Iceland officially became a sovereign state within the Kingdom of Iceland, marking a significant milestone in its history.

1944 - PRESENT

The story of Iceland's history, spanning from 1944 to the present day, is a compelling tale of substantial political, economic, and social transformations. This serves as an introduction to the chronicle of Iceland's journey through time, starting from 1944 up to the present day.

RECAP OF ICELAND'S INDEPENDENCE (1944)

The year 1944 holds a significant place for Iceland. It was on June 17, 1944, that Iceland broke away from the reins of Denmark, marking the birth of the Republic of Iceland. This monumental decision was not made in isolation but was a consequence of the tumultuous times during World War II.

Denmark, the country that had held sovereignty over Iceland, fell under the occupation of Nazi Germany. This event stirred a wave of concern about the future of Iceland's sovereignty. The shadow of uncertainty and the desire for self-governance led the people of Iceland to establish themselves as an independent republic.

Thus, the period around 1944 was a pivotal chapter in Iceland's history, marking its transition from being under Danish rule to standing as an independent nation. The echoes of this period continue to resonate in the proud and independent Republic of Iceland we know today.

POST-WORLD WAR II RECONSTRUCTION IN ICELAND

At the onset of World War II, Iceland was a sovereign kingdom in personal union with Denmark, with King Christian X as head of state. Despite officially remaining neutral throughout the war, Iceland was invaded by the British on May 10, 1940. The defence of Iceland was transferred from Britain to the United States on July 7, 1941, which was still a neutral country until five months later.

THE ARRIVAL OF US TROOPS IN ICELAND IN 1941

After the war, Iceland focused on rebuilding its economy, which was primarily based on fishing and agriculture. The country faced the daunting task of revitalising its economy and infrastructure that had been affected during the war years.

In 1948, Iceland benefited from the Marshall Plan, officially known as the European Recovery Program. This groundbreaking initiative played a pivotal role in the post-World War II reconstruction of war-ravaged Europe. The Marshall Plan aimed to revitalise the economies of European nations, foster regional stability, and promote lasting peace.

The primary goal of the Marshall Plan was to provide financial assistance for rebuilding Europe's shattered economies. The United States offered substantial financial aid to European countries, including Iceland, enabling them to invest in infrastructure, industrial production, and agricultural development.

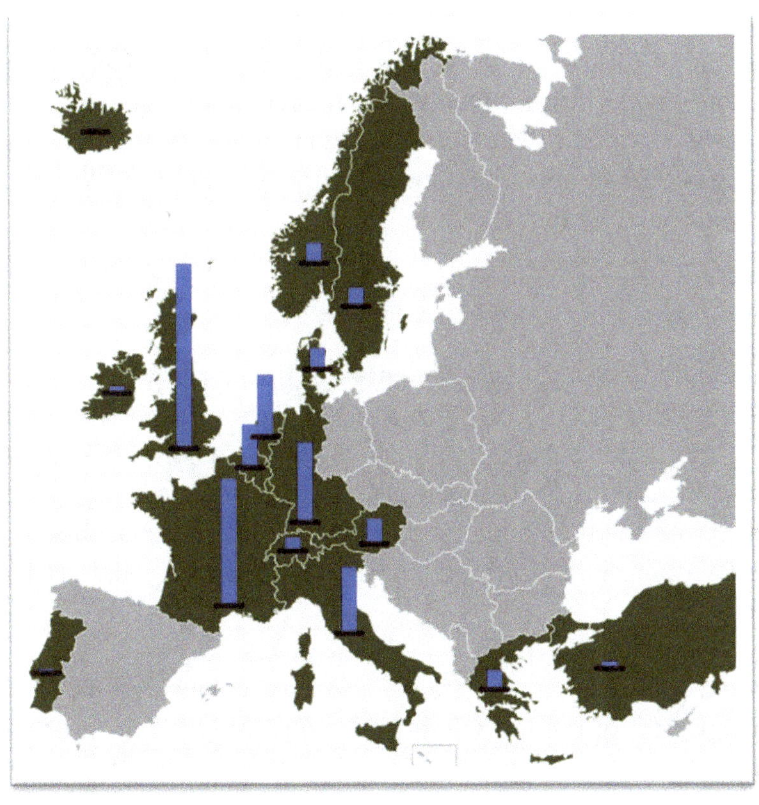

MAP SHOWING THE EUROPEAN RECOVERY PROGRAM AREAS

The Marshall Plan operated from 1948 to 1951, providing approximately $13 billion (equivalent to around $130 billion today) in economic aid to 16 European nations. The funds were used for a wide range of purposes, including rebuilding infrastructure, modernising industries, and supporting agricultural development.

The impact of the Marshall Plan extended far beyond its immediate economic objectives. It successfully jump-started Europe's recovery, leading to the emergence of robust economies that would become vital partners in the global arena. Moreover, the plan's focus on fostering stability and preventing the spread of communism played a crucial role in shaping the post-war political landscape.

The post-World War II reconstruction period in Iceland was marked by significant economic recovery and development, largely facilitated by the aid received through the Marshall Plan. This period laid the foundation for the prosperous and stable Iceland we know today.

COLD WAR ERA

Iceland became a founding member of the North Atlantic Treaty Organisation (NATO) on April 4, 1949. This membership, along with the 1951 bilateral Defence Agreement with the United States, formed the two main pillars of Iceland's security policy. Despite having no standing armed forces, Iceland contributed to NATO operations with financial contributions and civilian personnel.

Iceland operates an air defence and surveillance system (IADS) which is part of the NATO integrated Air Defence System. NATO conducts air-surveillance missions in Iceland as decided by the Alliance's North Atlantic Council in July of 2007.

The United States established a military base at Keflavík in 1951. This base, known as the Naval Air Station Keflavik (NASKEF), was located on the Reykjanes peninsula on the south-west portion of the island. The base was built during World War II by the United States Army as part of its mission to maintain the defence of Iceland and secure northern Atlantic air routes. It served to ferry personnel, equipment, and supplies to Europe.

The base was regularly visited by the American military and other NATO allies for military exercises, NATO Air Policing, and other tasks. The base remained operational until September 8, 2006. However, US forces returned to Keflavik in 2016, renovating parts of the base to accommodate P-8As on short duration/expeditionary detachments.

These strategic decisions positioned Iceland as a key player in the Cold War, aligning itself with Western powers and playing a crucial role in maintaining the balance of power during this tense period of global history.

THE NATO BASE AT KEFLAVIK AIRPORT

ECONOMIC GROWTH AND INDUSTRIALISATION

Iceland's economic growth has been both significantly higher and more volatile than in other OECD countries. The average annual growth rate of GDP from 1945 to 2007 was about 4%. The economy history of Iceland covers the development of its economy from the Settlement of Iceland in the late 9th century until the present.

FISHING INDUSTRY DEVELOPMENT

From the settlement of Iceland in the late 9th century until the 20th century, Iceland's economy rested on farming and fisheries. Since the 14th Century, fish products have been Iceland's most important export. The introduction of motorised vessels at the beginning of the 20th century revolutionised Icelandic fisheries.

As the fishing capacity grew, so did the total catch. In 2021 the overall catch amounted to 1,158,000 tons, and of that, 473,000 tons was the demersal species. The export value of marine products in 2021 was a total of ISK 296 billion (ISK refers to the Icelandic krónur), or 38.8% of the total export.

COD WARS

The Cod Wars were a series of confrontations in the mid-20th century between Iceland and the United Kingdom. The root of these conflicts lay in the rich cod fishing grounds surrounding Iceland, a resource that was vital to both nations.

In the 1950s, 1960s, and 1970s, Iceland found itself at odds with the UK and other countries due to disputes over fishing rights. The crux of the issue was Iceland's decision to extend its exclusive fishing zone, a move that was seen as an attempt to assert control over a larger area of the sea and protect its vital fishing industry.

The Cod Wars were not just about fish; they were also about national sovereignty, economic survival, and the rule of international law. The disputes led to diplomatic standoffs, aggressive naval manoeuvres, and even the severing of diplomatic ties.

Despite the tension and conflict, the Cod Wars ultimately led to a greater understanding of the importance of sustainable fishing and the need for international cooperation in managing shared resources.

CONFLICT ON THE HIGH SEAS BETWEEN ICELAND AND THE UK

Today, the Cod Wars serve as a reminder of the complex interplay between national interests, international law, and the need for sustainable practices in the fishing industry.

Iceland, a country known for its stable democratic governance since gaining independence, has a rich political history marked by regular elections and peaceful transitions of power. The political landscape of Iceland is characterised by the active participation of various political parties. Notably, the Independence Party, the Progressive Party, and the Social Democratic Alliance have played significant roles in shaping the country's governance.

Iceland's political system operates within the framework of a parliamentary representative democratic republic. The President serves as the head of state, while the Prime Minister acts as the head of government in a multi-party system. The executive power is exercised by the government, and legislative power is vested in both the government and the parliament, known as the Althing. The judiciary operates independently of the executive and the legislature.

CURRENT PRESIDENT OF ICELAND GUÐNI THORLACIUS JÓHANNESSON

As of 2024, the President of Iceland is Guðni Thorlacius Jóhannesson, who has been in office since August 1, 2016. The Prime Minister is Bjarni Benediktsson of the Independence Party.

Iceland's constitution, adopted in 1944, established a parliamentary democracy with a directly elected president as head of state. The powers of the president are similar to those of other heads of state in western European democracies.

Historically, Iceland has been governed by various coalitions formed by these parties. The coalition government is usually formed by the leaders of the political parties after discussions on which parties can form the cabinet and how its seats are to be distributed.

Iceland's political history is marked by its status as arguably the world's oldest assembly democracy. It has been rated as a "full democracy" in 2021. This democratic stability has been a cornerstone of Iceland's political developments since independence.

Iceland's political developments are characterised by its stable democratic governance, the active role of various political parties, and the peaceful transitions of power. This has resulted in a political environment that is conducive to the growth and prosperity of the nation.

FINANCIAL CRISIS (2008)

The financial crisis of 2008 had a profound impact on Iceland, leading to significant economic and political upheaval. This crisis was characterised by the default of all three of the country's major privately owned commercial banks, namely Kaupthing, Landsbanki, and Glitnir.

As the global financial crisis unfolded, investors began to perceive the Icelandic banks as increasingly risky. This led to a sharp depreciation of the Icelandic króna in 2008 and increased difficulties for the banks in rolling over their short-term debt. By the end of the second quarter of 2008, Iceland's external debt was equal to more than 11 times the national GDP.

THE THREE ICELANDIC BANKS IN CRISIS

A decade later, Iceland has risen from the wreckage of the banking crisis. The turnaround has been relatively fast, with the country returning to growth in 2011. The GDP growth rate exceeds 7%, among the highest in the world. The World Bank Group notes that GDP has bounced back from a 2009 low of $12.9 billion to more than $20 billion today.

A key driver of this recovery has been the tourism industry. At the beginning of the 2000s, around 300 thousand foreigners visited Iceland. However, by the end of the 2010s, the number had climbed above two million – nearly six times the Icelandic population. Tourism provides 39% of Iceland's annual export revenue and contributes about 10% to the country's GDP. It accounts for 15% of the workforce, and in 2017, 47% of Iceland's newest jobs were in some way related to the tourism industry.

The government played a crucial role in this growth by establishing a brand-new Tourist Control Centre, which coordinates the government's work in tourism nationwide. It also implemented efforts to track the most popular tourist destinations and receive input from tourists on how to improve their experiences at those destinations.

Iceland's recovery from the financial crisis and the subsequent growth of its tourism industry is a testament to the country's resilience and strategic planning. It offers valuable lessons for other countries on how to deal with a financial downturn and bounce back. However, while the country's economic recovery has been strong, it continues to face political and judicial challenges.

CLIMATE CHANGE AND ITS IMPACT

THE JÖKULSÁRLÓN GLACIER LAGOON

Climate change has had a profound impact on Iceland's natural landscapes, particularly its glaciers. The effects of global warming are increasingly visible in Iceland as the landscape begins to radically alter. For instance, the world-famous Jökulsárlón Lagoon in Iceland, which contains icebergs as far as the eye can see, carries a very alarming message with its drifting pieces of melting ice.

Iceland's glaciers, which cover roughly 10% of the island, are melting so fast that it's creating problems for the guiding companies. In fact, it's predicted that Iceland could be iceless by 2200. This rapid melting of glaciers is expected to have a major impact on the country's industries, from fishing to tourism.

RENEWABLE ENERGY AND CLIMATE CHANGE EFFORTS

Iceland is a world leader in renewable energy. The country meets 85% of its primary energy needs with indigenous renewable resources. Almost all electricity in Iceland is produced using renewable energy sources, with 73% provided by hydropower plants and 26.8% from geothermal energy.

In terms of climate change, Iceland aims to achieve carbon neutrality before 2040 and to cut greenhouse gas emissions by 40% by 2030 under the Paris Agreement. The country has a Climate Action Plan, updated in 2020, which contains 48 actions and is Iceland's main policy instrument to reach its goals of cutting emissions and reaching carbon neutrality.

PUBLIC AWARENESS AND GOVERNMENT INITIATIVES

Icelanders have become increasingly aware of and concerned about environmental issues since the turn of the century. A majority of Icelanders believe that the government is not doing enough to limit greenhouse gas emissions in the country.

Environmental issues rank among what Icelanders see as their country's top five challenges.

In response, the government has been investing millions of euros to increase carbon sequestration and accelerate switches to sustainable energy sources. Iceland aims to go carbon neutral by 2040.

While Iceland has made significant strides in harnessing renewable energy and addressing environmental challenges, the impact of climate change on its natural landscapes, particularly its glaciers, remains a pressing concern. The country continues to explore innovative solutions and policies to mitigate these issues and transition towards a more sustainable future.

THE GOVERNMENT CLIMATE ACTION PLAN PUBLISHED

GENDER EQUALITY IN ICELAND

Iceland is a global leader in gender equality. The country has consistently ranked first in the World Economic Forum's Global Gender Gap Index. This achievement is a testament to the collective action and solidarity of women human rights defenders, political will, and tools such as legislation, gender budgeting, and quotas. The country's legislation on gender equality includes the Act on Equal Status and Equal Rights Irrespective of Gender and the Act on the Administration of Matters Concerning Equality.

PRESERVATION OF CULTURAL HERITAGE

THE NATIONAL MUSEUM OF ICELAND IN REYKJAVIK

The Cultural Heritage Act in Iceland promotes the protection of the country's cultural heritage and ensures its preservation. The National Museum of Iceland is the centre for the preservation of

Icelandic national heritage. The country also has numerous heritage museums, district museums, and museums dedicated to special fields throughout the country.

IMMIGRATION

Iceland is a member of the Schengen Area, which allows free movement of people between member states. The country has representation agreements with nine other Schengen Member States for processing applications for a Schengen visa to Iceland. The Directorate of Immigration processes applications for residence permits, Icelandic citizenship, international protection, and visas.

SPORTING ACHIEVEMENTS

Iceland's national football team made waves during the 2016 Euro by reaching the quarter-finals. Their passionate fans, the famous "Viking Clap," and the team's resilient performance captured global attention. Eiður Guðjohnsen was former Chelsea and Barcelona forward is Iceland's all-time leading goal scorer, with 24 goals in 74 matches.

Iceland's men's handball team consistently competes at the highest level. They have participated in multiple World Championships and European Championships, often causing upsets against stronger opponents.

The women's handball team has also achieved success, qualifying for major tournaments and showcasing their skill and determination.

Despite its small population, Iceland has produced talented winter athletes. From cross-country skiing to snowboarding,

Icelandic athletes have represented their country in international competitions.

FOOTBALLER EIÐUR GUÐJOHNSEN

ICELANDIC MUSIC

Icelandic music has journeyed through diverse landscapes since the nation's independence in 1944. From the revival of folk melodies to the global resonance of contemporary artists, Icelandic music reflects both the resilience of its cultural roots and the dynamism of its creative spirit.

The post-independence era witnessed a revival of Icelandic folk music, as artists like Þrjú Menn í Bíti and Spilverk Þjóðanna endeavoured to preserve and celebrate the nation's musical heritage. This resurgence set the stage for the exploration of new sounds in the subsequent decades.

During the 1960s and 1970s, Icelandic pop and rock bands emerged, drawing inspiration from international trends while infusing their music with Icelandic lyrics and themes. Acts like Hljómar and Trúbrot captivated audiences with their energetic performances, laying the groundwork for the burgeoning music scene.

The 1980s marked a pivotal period with the rise of punk and alternative music in Iceland. Influential bands such as Purrkur Pillnikk and Kuki, featuring Björk, challenged conventions and sparked a cultural revolution. Björk's subsequent solo career propelled Icelandic music onto the global stage, showcasing the country's avant-garde spirit and innovative approach.

SINGER/SONGWRITER BJÖRK

As the new millennium dawned, Icelandic music continued to evolve, embracing a diverse array of genres and styles. Post-rock pioneers Sigur Rós captivated audiences with their ethereal soundscapes, while experimental artists like múm and Jóhann Jóhannsson pushed the boundaries of sonic exploration.

The 2010s witnessed the emergence of Icelandic pop and indie acts reaching international acclaim. Of Monsters and Men, with their infectious folk-pop anthems, and Ásgeir, with his haunting melodies, captured the hearts of audiences worldwide. Simultaneously, the electronic and dance music scene flourished, with acts like GusGus and FM Belfast electrifying stages both at home and abroad.

Icelandic music from 1944 to the present day encapsulates a journey of resilience, innovation, and creative exploration. From the revival of folk traditions to the global impact of contemporary artists, Icelandic musicians have continually pushed boundaries, defying expectations and captivating audiences around the world.

SUMMARY:

Iceland's journey from 1944 to the present day is a tale of resilience, transformation, and innovation across political, economic, social, and cultural spheres. The nation's declaration of independence from Denmark in 1944 marked a pivotal moment, leading to post-war reconstruction efforts supported by initiatives like the Marshall Plan. The Cold War era saw Iceland aligning with Western powers and hosting strategic military bases.

Economic growth, driven by fishing industry development and post-crisis recovery, was complemented by the rise of tourism. However, challenges such as the Cod Wars and the 2008 financial crisis tested Iceland's resilience. Environmental concerns, particularly regarding climate change and glacier melt, have spurred efforts towards renewable energy and sustainability.

Iceland's commitment to gender equality, immigration policies, cultural preservation, and sporting achievements have also shaped its identity on the global stage. Through it all, Icelandic music has mirrored the nation's journey, blending tradition with innovation and captivating audiences worldwide.

PEOPLE:

Sveinn Björnsson (1881-1952): First President of Iceland (1944-1952), played a crucial role in Iceland's independence from Denmark.

Halldór Laxness (1902-1998): Renowned Icelandic writer, awarded the Nobel Prize in Literature in 1955.

Vigdís Finnbogadóttir (b. 1930): Iceland's first female president (1980-1996), and the world's first democratically elected female president.

Jónas Árnason (1923-2004): A prominent politician, served as Prime Minister of Iceland from 1987 to 1988.

Björk Guðmundsdóttir (b. 1965): Internationally acclaimed singer-songwriter, known simply as Björk.

Eiður Guðjohnsen (b. 1978): An Icelandic footballer having enjoyed a successful career at clubs such as Chelsea, Barcelona, and Bolton Wanderers, as well as representing Iceland internationally.

PLACES:

Reykjavík: The capital and largest city of Iceland, where most of the political and cultural activities take place.

Thingvellir National Park: A UNESCO World Heritage Site, significant for its geological and historical importance, including being the site of Iceland's first parliament, the Althing.

Eyjafjallajökull: A glacier-capped volcano in southern Iceland, known for its 2010 eruption that disrupted air travel across Europe.

Declaration of Independence (1944): Iceland declared independence from Denmark on June 17, 1944, establishing the Republic of Iceland with Sveinn Björnsson as its first president.

Cod Wars (1950s-1970s): Series of confrontations between Iceland and the United Kingdom over fishing rights in the North Atlantic, with Iceland asserting control over its territorial waters.

Icelandic Financial Crisis (2006-2011): A severe economic downturn that resulted in the collapse of Iceland's banking system, leading to political unrest and significant reforms in the financial sector.

Gender Equality Movement: Iceland has been at the forefront of promoting gender equality, with significant progress made in closing the gender pay gap and increasing female representation in politics and other sectors.

Ingólfr Arnarson (c. 874 – c. 950): Often considered the first permanent settler of Iceland, Ingólfr Arnarson is credited with establishing the first settlement in Reykjavik around 874.

Snorri Sturluson (1179 – 1241): A prominent Icelandic historian, poet, and politician, Snorri Sturluson is best known for his contributions to Old Norse literature, particularly his prose Edda and the Heimskringla sagas.

Hákon IV Hákonarson (1204 – 1263): Hákon IV, also known as Hákon the Old, was a Norwegian king who exerted significant influence over Iceland during his reign. He played a role in establishing Norwegian authority over the island.

Jón Sigurðsson (1811 – 1879): A key figure in Iceland's struggle for independence from Denmark, Jón Sigurðsson was a statesman and scholar who advocated for Icelandic cultural and political autonomy.

Christian IX (1818 – 1906): As the King of Denmark from 1863 to 1906, Christian IX was also the King of Iceland during Denmark's rule over the island. He signed the Constitution of Iceland in 1874, granting Iceland limited home rule.

Hannes Hafstein (1861 – 1922): Iceland's first Minister for Iceland from 1904 to 1909, Hannes Hafstein played a significant role in Iceland's path towards independence. He was also a poet and writer.

King Frederick VIII (1843 – 1912): Frederick VIII succeeded Christian IX as King of Denmark and, by extension, King of Iceland. He reigned from 1906 to 1912.

King Christian X (1870 – 1947): Christian X, who reigned from 1912 to 1947, was the last monarch to rule over Iceland before it became a republic. His reign saw significant changes in Iceland's relationship with Denmark.

Sveinn Björnsson (1881 – 1952): Iceland's first president, Sveinn Björnsson, served from 1944 until his death in 1952. He played a crucial role in Iceland's transition from a monarchy to a republic.

Ásgeir Ásgeirsson (1894 – 1972): Ásgeir Ásgeirsson served as the second President of Iceland, succeeding Sveinn Björnsson. He held office from 1952 to 1968.

Kristján Eldjárn (1916 – 1982): Kristján Eldjárn, a historian and politician, served as the third President of Iceland from 1968 to 1980.

Vigdís Finnbogadóttir (b. 1930): Iceland's first female president, Vigdís Finnbogadóttir, served as the fourth President of Iceland from 1980 to 1996, making her the world's first democratically elected female president.

Ólafur Ragnar Grímsson (b. 1943): Ólafur Ragnar Grímsson served as the fifth President of Iceland from 1996 to 2016, making him one of the longest-serving Icelandic presidents.

Guðni Thorlacius Jóhannesson (b. 1968): Guðni Thorlacius. Jóhannesson has been serving as the sixth President of Iceland since 2016, succeeding Ólafur Ragnar Grímsson.

Serbia Through the Ages (2023) ISBN: 9786197742374		**26 Tales of Humanities Trials** (2023) ISBN 9786199249482	
Simple Treasures in Bulgaria (2008) ISBN 9780955984907		**I'm Bad at Poems** (2022) ISBN 9786199249420	
Wales Through the Ages (2023) ISBN 9786197742336		**Redemption of Love** (2023) ISBN 9786199249406	
100 Essential Recipes from Bulgaria (2011) ISBN 9781447702603		**Romania Through the Ages** (2023) ISBN 9786197742190	
North Macedonia Through the Ages (2023) ISBN 9786197742251		**Cyprus Through the Ages** (2023) ISBN 9786197742220